Contents

HELLO WORLD!

Grab your pens and pencils to fill in these pages with everything about YOU!

My name is ....

I am .... years old

3 words that describe me:

My best friends are . . .

....

....

....

....

What do you prefer?

(Circle your favorites from each option.)

Sweet / Savory

TV shows / Movies

Writing / Math

Sport / Art

Dog / Cat

Indoor / Outdoor

Summer / Winter

Growth Mindset Ninja
ACTIVITY BOOK

Ninja Life Hacks™

Welcome

Hello there, ninjas! I'm Growth Mindset Ninja and this is my activity book. It's packed with everything from puzzles to coloring and fill-in fun!

This book belongs to

....

....

Having a growth mindset is about the power of possibility.

FEELING DISCOURAGED?

That's okay. It's totally normal to feel frustrated when you struggle with a task, or things don't go to plan. Inside this book, you will find new ways to cope when things go wrong and you want to give up. As well as fun puzzles, you will find useful tips, mindfulness activities, and breathing techniques. The coolest thing is that you can take these skills wherever you go—they can be your secret weapon to overcoming anything!

THIS IS MY FAMILY.

Draw them in this picture frame.

Ninja Life Hacks™

All about me!

DRAW A CHECK NEXT TO THE THINGS YOU LIKE TO DO, THEN WRITE YOUR OWN IN THE BLANK SPACES.

I am good at . . .

- ☐ Art
- ☐ Math
- ☐ Spelling
- ☐ Sport
- ☐ Gymnastics
- ☐ Dancing

_____
_____
_____

- ☐ Bake
- ☐ Cycle
- ☐ Draw
- ☐ Run
- ☐ Play sport
- ☐ Swim

_____
_____
_____
_____
_____

When I am good at something I feel . . .

- ☐ Proud
- ☐ Happy
- ☐ Strong
- ☐ Smart
- ☐ Confident

CAN YOU REMEMBER A TIME WHEN YOU DID SOMETHING REALLY WELL?

Draw a picture of it in this space.
Perhaps you learned to ride your bike, or earned an award. It can be whatever you like!

All about me!

CIRCLE THE THINGS THAT YOU DON'T LIKE TO DO, THEN WRITE YOUR OWN IN THE SPACES.

Bake

Dance

Play video games

Swim

Paint

Skateboard

Read

....
....
....
....
....
....
....

I am not very good at...

Art   Sport

Math   Gymnastics

Spelling   Dancing

....
....
....
....
....
....
....
....
....

YET!

- ☐ Frustrated
- ☐ Angry
- ☐ Sad
- ☐ Stressed
- ☐ Shy
- ☐ Anxious
- ☐ Determined–I want to learn!
- ☐ Fine–we can't be good at everything!

Sport

Keeping a diary

Cooking or baking

Trying new things

Running

Tidying my room

Spelling

Reading

COLOR IN A STAR NEXT TO THE THINGS YOU WOULD LIKE TO GET BETTER AT. YOU CAN WRITE YOUR OWN ON THE DOTTED LINES!

SECRET WEAPON

When Growth Mindset Ninja wants to do something, they focus on the task and see it through to the finish. Grab your colors and finish the picture like Growth Mindset Ninja.

How did this activity make YOU feel?

Add a thumbs-up or a thumbs-down sticker here. →

I DON'T KNOW HOW TO . . .

YET! Complete the sentences by filling in the blanks with things you would like to learn or get better at.

IDEAS:
I DON'T KNOW HOW TO DANCE YET.
I CAN'T RIDE A BIKE YET.

I don't know how to .... YET

I'm no good at .... YET

I can't .... YET

I don't know if I can .... YET

I haven't tried .... YET

I can't master .... YET

PICTURE SUCCESS

Imagine achieving your dream! What would the moment look like? Draw it in the space.

Impulsive Ninja

Integrity Ninja

PERHAPS YOU WANT TO LEARN TO PLAY THE GUITAR OR SKATEBOARD—IT'S UP TO YOU!

ORANGE OR GREEN?

Color in all of the things that you can do in green, and then color in all of the things you can't do yet in orange. Write your own in the blank stars—these can be things you can do or goals you want to achieve.

Ride a bike

Say the alphabet backwards

Can do

Can't do yet

Dive

Roller skate

Breakdance

Swim

Count to 10 in a different language

Balance on one leg

Sing

Use a calculator

Cartwheel

I can't handstand yet, but I'd really like to!

Play a musical instrument

Bake cookies

Run

Surf

Handstand

Count to 100

Speak a second language

Dance

Jump rope

DON'T WORRY IF YOUR PAGE LOOKS REALLY ORANGE. IT JUST MEANS YOU HAVE LOTS OF FUN THINGS TO LOOK FORWARD TO TRYING OUT!

TANGLED LINES

Growth Mindset Ninja's father took them fishing, but the lines got all tangled up. Growth Mindset Ninja was frustrated but their dad said, "You just haven't caught the fish . . . yet!" Which one leads to the fish?

ODD FISH OUT

Growth Mindset Ninja loves fishing and seeing all the colorful fish in the lake. Can you find the odd one out in each row? Circle your answers.

1

 A

 B

 C

 D

2

 A

 B

 C

3

 A

 B

 C

I believed I could do it, and look what happened!

How did this activity make YOU feel?

Add a thumbs-up or a thumbs-down sticker here. →

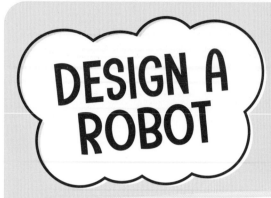

DESIGN A ROBOT

Growth Mindset Ninja can't get the robot to work. Design a new one together as a team! Draw it in the space and don't forget to add some color.

ROBOT NAME: . . . .

I need some help!

WHAT CAN YOUR ROBOT DO?

WRITE DOWN WHAT IT CAN DO. MAYBE IT COULD DO THE CHORES FOR YOU!

DRAW SOME COOL GADGETS FOR YOUR ROBOT! DOES IT LIGHT UP OR HAVE A SPECIAL ARM FOR REACHING HIGH UP THINGS?

Ninja Life Hacks

BIG BRAIN

Growth Mindset Ninja knows that "yet," can turn the impossible into possible and help your brain find answers to problems. Color in and decorate this poster, then cut it out and hang it up on a wall so you always remember the magic word!

TONS OF TOYS

Hard-Working Ninja is finding it tricky to sort out the toys, but will the magic word of "yet" help? Draw lines to match up the toys to the correct shadow.

How did this activity make YOU feel?

Add a thumbs-up or a thumbs-down sticker here. →

JUST BREATHE

Taking a break is important! These ninjas are enjoying some calming yoga together. Look carefully at the picture and then try the fun quiz.

CAN YOU SPOT THIS FOOTBALL IN THE BIG PICTURE?

HOW MANY NINJAS ARE IN THE SCENE ALTOGETHER? DRAW A CHECK NEXT TO THE CORRECT NUMBER.

⬜ 6   ⬜ 8   ⬜ 10

TRUE OR FALSE? COLOR IN T FOR TRUE OR F FOR FALSE TO COMPLETE THESE ANSWERS.

CIRCLE ALL 6 THINGS THAT ARE MISSING FROM THE BIG PICTURE.

1. There are 3 yellow ninjas in the scene.

T   F

2. One ninja is not using a mat.

T   F

3. All the ninjas look calm.

T   F

MAKE IT MATCH

Gritty Ninja isn't good at everything, but they succeed because they never give up. There are 6 differences between picture A and picture B. Draw in what is missing to make the two pictures match!

B

Add a growth mindset sticker below for every difference you spot.

WORD SEARCH

Growth Mindset Ninja knows that mistakes are all part of learning. Can you find all of these encouraging words in the grid?

F	W	H	U	P	B	H	D	S	Z	P	C	S	W	E
U	G	V	X	B	A	T	N	V	A	G	Y	J	K	M
S	E	Q	Z	E	J	L	U	C	Z	B	Z	P	Y	L
B	N	U	W	L	I	A	P	R	A	C	T	I	C	E
P	C	Q	M	I	N	B	V	C	M	A	S	M	Y	A
K	O	Y	B	E	C	X	Z	N	B	L	H	P	A	R
L	U	K	J	V	H	G	F	D	I	A	M	R	N	N
V	R	L	K	E	H	G	F	D	T	D	C	O	U	I
O	A	W	Y	H	B	K	S	K	I	A	P	V	N	N
O	G	N	H	F	R	S	O	A	O	H	U	E	J	G
W	E	Q	C	H	A	L	L	E	N	G	E	W	E	R
P	O	I	U	T	I	D	V	C	V	V	B	N	M	W
M	H	T	F	V	N	X	E	D	H	C	Z	C	V	L
E	R	T	Y	U	I	O	H	F	D	S	I	O	M	A
I	F	S	U	C	C	E	S	S	R	Y	J	V	C	A

- ☐ AMBITION
- ☐ CHALLENGE
- ☐ BRAIN
- ☐ PRACTICE
- ☐ LEARNING
- ☐ ENCOURAGE
- ☐ SOLVE
- ☐ BELIEVE
- ☐ SUCCESS
- ☐ IMPROVE

FEELING GOOD

There's no better feeling than when you achieve something you worked hard at! Write the correct letters in the spaces to complete this jigsaw.

A

B

C

D

E

CAN'T DO THIS

It can feel tough when you can't do something! Fill the raindrops with words to describe how you feel when you fail or can't figure something out.

IDEAS: FRUSTRATED, TIRED, ANGRY

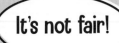

It's not fair!

CAN DO THIS

It can feel incredible when you are good at something! Fill the stars with words to describe how you feel when you succeed.

IDEAS: PROUD, HAPPY, CONFIDENT

I feel like a superhero!

How did this activity make YOU feel?

Add a thumbs-up or a thumbs-down sticker here.

29

WHAT A MESS

Growth Mindset Ninja used to feel bad when things didn't go as planned. Now they know that learning is part of the fun! Can you spot 8 differences between picture A and picture B?

WHAT A MESS

Growth Mindset Ninja used to feel bad when things didn't go as planned. Now they know that learning is part of the fun! Can you spot 8 differences between picture A and picture B?

CAN DO THIS

It can feel incredible when you are good at something! Fill the stars with words to describe how you feel when you succeed.

IDEAS: PROUD, HAPPY, CONFIDENT

I feel like a superhero!

How did this activity make YOU feel?

Add a thumbs-up or a thumbs-down sticker here. →

29

Add a growth mindset sticker below for every difference you spot.

LET'S GROW

Can you think of any words or phrases about growth? Write them in the blank spaces to complete this puzzle.

G
....

R
....

O
....

W
....

T
....

H
....

HERE ARE SOME IDEAS FOR INSPIRATION!

O _vercome_

challenges

W _ise_

How did this activity make YOU feel?

Add a thumbs-up or a thumbs-down sticker here. →

BREATHING WAND

Deep breathing can calm us down when things feel out of control. Create a mindfulness breathing wand to help you slow down, relax, and find your inner peace!

YOU WILL NEED:
- [ ] Cardboard tube
- [ ] Crayons, pens, or paint
- [ ] Safe scissors
- [ ] Colorful tissue paper
- [ ] Sticky tape

ASK A GROWNUP TO HELP YOU.

HOW TO MAKE IT:

1. Decorate your cardboard tube using crayons or pens.

2. Snip your tissue paper into strips.

3. Then tape them to the end of the cardboard tube.

4. Blow through the tube calmly for 3 seconds to watch the tissue pieces flutter.

My breathing wand helps me feel relaxed.

TURN IT AROUND

Worries are a normal part of life, but having a positive mindset can help you get past them. What do you worry about? Color in or write down your worries in the red clouds below, then turn them into positives in the blue clouds.

I can't ride a bike

I'm bad at making friends

My homework is too hard

I'm no good at running

I can't climb the jungle gym

COOKERY DISASTER

Growth Mindset Ninja is having a cooking disaster. Write down helpful things in the speech bubbles to encourage them.

KEEP CALM

Anxious Ninja is panicking and lost in a maze! Show them the way to the finish by following the sequence below. Follow the symbols in the order below to find your way through the maze.

YOU CAN MOVE UP, DOWN AND ACROSS, BUT NOT DIAGONALLY

START HERE

How will I ever find the way?!

FINISH

37

DRAW YOUR SUCCESS

Is there something you've ALWAYS wanted to be able to do but can't yet? Draw or write about it here.

IT COULD BE LEARNING TO DIVE, PERFECTING YOUR BAKING, OR LEARNING YOUR TIMES TABLES.

DRAW YOUR DREAM HERE

NOW CLOSE YOUR EYES AND IMAGINE SUCCEEDING. THINK ABOUT HOW IT MAKES YOU FEEL.

DRAW YOUR FACE HERE

POSITIVE AFFIRMATIONS

Words are powerful and can change how we feel! Scribble down some positive phrases to look back at when you're faced with a tricky challenge.

HOW ABOUT THESE TO GET YOU STARTED?

I am going to do this

I am stronger than I realize

I am determined

I am able to get through this

I am going to try my best

GROW MY MIND

Having a growth mindset is about looking for positive ways to learn and try new things. It's not about putting pressure on yourself to be great at everything! Use this space to record the things you are good at and the things you'd like to explore more.

COLOR IN THE THINGS YOU'RE GOOD AT FROM THE CHOICES AND WRITE YOUR OWN IN THE SPACES.

Rock climbing

Reading

Gymnastics

Swimming

Dancing

Drawing

Baking

Writing

Spelling

Math

Painting

Gardening

I'm Positive Ninja and I like to focus on what I CAN do.

Baking

Math

Gymnastics

COLOR IN WHAT YOU'D LIKE TO IMPROVE OR DO MORE OF IN THE FUTURE.

Writing

Spelling

Reading

Painting

Dancing

Drawing

Swimming

Rock climbing

Gardening

I'm Ambitious Ninja and I love to focus on what I WILL do.

How did this activity make YOU feel?

Add a thumbs-up or a thumbs-down sticker here.

FUN AT THE FAIR

Fairground rides can be scary, but a growth mindset encourages the ninjas to give new things a try! Can you find the odd one out in each row? Add a sticker next to your answer.

1

A   B   C   D

2

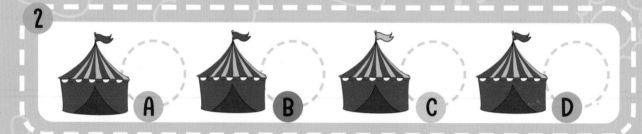

A   B   C   D

3

A   B   C   D

I am nervous about going on the big rides, but I might enjoy it!

CRACK THE CODE

Can you help Growth Mindset Ninja reveal these secret codes? Use the key to help you figure out what the symbols spell out.

▲	■	☾	★	■	●	▲	☾	⬡	●	●	★	★
A	B	C	D	E	F	G	H	I	J	K	L	M

◆	▲	☾	★	■	▲	☾	⬡	▲	◆	☾	◆
N	O	P	Q	R	S	T	U	V	W	X	Y	Z

_ _ _ _ _ _ _ _ _ _

_ _ _ _ _ _ _ _ _ _

_ _ _ _ _ _ _ _ _ _ _

_ _ _ _ _ _ _ _ _ _ _ _ _ _ _

43

ALL ABOUT THE ATTITUDE

Growth mindset is a belief that you can become good at something with more practice. It's the opposite of a fixed mindset, which is a belief that if you're not good at something at first, you never will be.

Look at all these phrases and color in the fixed mindset red and the growth mindset green!

Learning is part of the fun

I love trying new things

GROWTH MINDSET

FIXED MINDSET

I will try again

I will never be good at this

As long as I try my best, that's all that matters

I always fail

I'll get better

Mistakes are a waste of time

I will never get better at this

Mistakes are part of learning

I give up

I quit

I am improving

Being bad at something is ok, I'll just try my best

I can't do this yet

It doesn't bother me if I don't get something right away

I hate this

I haven't mastered that yet

It might be hard, but it'll be even more rewarding when I CAN do it!

Being bad at something makes me mad

How did this activity make YOU feel?

Add a thumbs-up or a thumbs-down sticker here. →

HOT CHOC

Find your inner calm by imagining you are holding a mug of hot chocolate. Simple breathing exercises like this one can help you take back control so you can tackle any challenge.

1. Breathe in through your nose to smell the hot chocolate.

2. Breathe slowly out through your mouth to cool it down.

3. Repeat this as many times as you like!

NOW COLOR IN THE DRINK USING YOUR FAVORITE COLORED PENCILS OR CRAYONS.

BRAIN BUILDING

A belief that anything is possible is Growth Mindset Ninja's secret weapon for building a strong brain! Finish this this picture using your brightest colors.

GROWTH MINDSET NINJA CAN'T SOLVE THIS PUZZLE... YET!

STRESS BUSTER

Life can get a bit much and we can put too much pressure on ourselves. This grid is packed with quick activities to give your brain a rest! So, take five minutes from your homework or whatever else you're doing and give these activities a try.

DO SOME STRETCHES	Balance on your left leg for as long as you can	Jump up and down on the spot for 20 seconds
Read a book for 10 minutes	Have a healthy snack	**CLOSE YOUR EYES FOR 5 MINUTES**
Lie on your back on the floor for 5 minutes		Hop for 20 seconds
Move your upper body for 20 seconds	Make 5 big circles with each arm	**HAVE A GLASS OF WATER**

PICK AN ACTIVITY FROM THE GRID. WHEN YOU'VE COMPLETED IT, COLOR THE SQUARE RED, YELLOW, BLUE, OR GREEN BASED ON HOW HELPFUL YOU FOUND IT. LOOK AT THE COLOR KEY FOR HELP!

Color Key

| Didn't like it/ Not helpful | It was ok | Feel calmer | Loved it! |

High knee running on the spot for 10 seconds

DO SOME MINDFUL COLORING

Try the hot choc breathing activity from page 46

GET SOME FRESH AIR

LISTEN TO YOUR FAVORITE SONG

Lie on your bed for 5 minutes

Spin for 10 seconds

Have a warm drink

Balance on one leg for as long as you can

How did this activity make YOU feel?

Add a thumbs-up or a thumbs-down sticker here.

COLOR RACE

Try this coloring game with a friend! Pick one ninja each to color in and take turns rolling the die. Whatever number a player lands on, they color in that section on their picture. First to complete their ninja wins!

YOU WILL NEED A DIE FOR THIS ACTIVITY

GROWTH MINDSET NINJA

AMBITIOUS
NINJA

SKATE ON

These ninjas know that it doesn't matter how good you are—it's trying your best that counts! Can you find each item from the panel below at the skate park? Add a sticker when you spot them.

GET MOVING

Being active improves focus and helps build self-esteem, so you're more likely to succeed. Spell out your name using this chart and complete each action as you go . . . all of them!

YOUR NAME: _____

A 10 jumping jacks

B March on the spot for 10 seconds

C Do 10 sit-ups

D Stand on one leg for as long as you can

E Wave your arms over your head

F Shuffle across the room on your bottom

G Hop 15 times

H Pick up a ball without using your hands

I Swing your arms from side to side

J Jump up as high as you can 8 times

K Wiggle your whole body for 5 seconds

L Run on the spot for 20 seconds

M Bend over and touch your toes

N Crawl around the room

O Dribble a ball

P Do your best twirl

Q Take 10 deep breaths

R Cartwheel

S Balance a soft toy on your head and try to walk around without it falling off

T Scribble on some blank paper

U Do a lap of the room on your knees

V Bend over and touch your toes

W Run on the spot for 30 seconds

X Do a silly dance

Y Walk into every room in your house

Z Move around like your favorite animal

Positive Ninja

Perfect Ninja

Hard-working Ninja

Creative Ninja

Brave Ninja

Shy Ninja

NOW FIND THE MONTH YOU WERE BORN. CIRCLE YOUR BIRTH MONTH AND DO THE ACTIVITY!

JANUARY — Curl up into a tiny ball

FEBRUARY — 10 star jumps

MARCH — Stand up and shake off your arms and legs

APRIL — Leap around like a frog

MAY — Slither on the floor like a snake

JUNE — Hop like a kangaroo

JULY — Try to moonwalk

AUGUST — Stand as still as you can for 2 minutes

SEPTEMBER — Move around slowly like a snail

OCTOBER — Wriggle like a caterpillar

NOVEMBER — Flap your arms like they're wings

DECEMBER — Make 5 big circles with each arm

How did this activity make YOU feel?

Add a thumbs-up or a thumbs-down sticker here.

Lazy Ninja

Ugh, do I have to?

Growth Mindset Ninja

Come on Lazy Ninja, it'll be good for you!

MATCHY MATCHY

Compassionate Ninja spent a long time teaching their dog a trick. See if you can figure out which little picture matches the big one.

COLOR BY NUMBERS

Growth Mindset Ninja is learning how to play baseball. With hard work, they know they will keep getting better! Use the color key to help you choose which colors to use on this picture.

BRAIN POWER

Learning ways to overcome challenges helped this ninja to grow the mightiest brain! Here are some tips to build yours, too.

Don't sit down for too long

Stand up tall and reach as high as you can

Have a glass of water

Write down 3 good things about today

Add "yet" when you talk about things you can't do

Spot 5 things of the same color in your house

Get some fresh air

Eat well

Do some big stretches

Try something new

Take a break

Go outside and try to spot five things in the sky

Do 10 jumping jacks

Try to find the fun in each challenge!

ADD A LIGHTBULB STICKER WHEN YOU TRY EACH IDEA.

MY GROWTH MINDSET JOURNAL

Journaling is a helpful mindfulness tool. You can log your growth mindset progress and see how far you've come! Each day write down at least one way that you practiced growth mindset.

Monday

....

....

Tuesday

....

....

Wednesday

....

....

I CAN'T DO BACKSTROKE . . . YET!

Thursday

....

....

Friday

....

....

I WASN'T AS FAST AS MY FRIENDS, BUT I WILL GET BETTER.

Saturday

....

....

Sunday

....

....

I COULDN'T SPELL A WORD, BUT I JUST TRIED AGAIN.

PAPER PLANE RACE

The ninjas are at the park playing with their paper planes. Follow the tangled paths to see whose plane reaches the finish first!

Compassionate Ninja

Calm Ninja

Helpful Ninja

Hardworking Ninja

SUDOKU

Creative Ninja is super curious and loves reading to find out about new things! Complete the grid using your stickers.

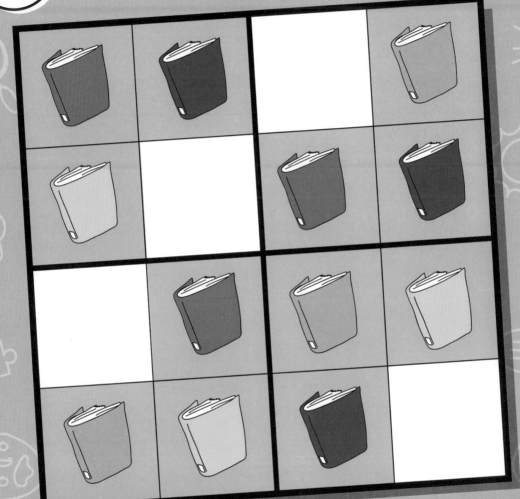

Reading helps me add to my knowledge.

REMEMBER THAT EACH BOOK MUST ONLY APPEAR ONCE IN EACH COLUMN AND ROW. GOOD LUCK!

MY MISSION

Setting goals is a fun way to grow your brain every day. Write 6 things you can't do, or you're not very good at, then add "YET" at the end of each one!

MY MISSION!

1 ....

2 ....

3 ....

4 ....

5 ....

6 ....

USE SOME OF THESE SUGGESTIONS OR MAKE UP YOUR OWN.

IDEAS

I can't skateboard YET

I'm not very good at spelling YET

I don't know how to play the piano YET

TRACE AND BREATHE

Focusing on nature can be a great way to find inner peace. Try this mindful breathing activity for ultimate calmness.

COLOR IN THIS LEAF USING A SHADE THAT YOU FIND CALMING. THEN, SLOWLY TRACE THE OUTLINE WITH A FINGER WHILE YOU BREATHE IN AND THEN OUT.

BREATHE IN

BREATHE OUT

How did this activity make YOU feel?

Add a thumbs-up or a thumbs-down sticker here.

GIVE IT A TRY

Who do you look up to? Pick 4 people that inspire you for a special talent they have and ask them to teach you. Write and draw about each person you admire below!

Good at: . . . . Will ask . . . .

Good at: . . . . Will ask . . . .

Good at: . . . . Will ask . . . .

Good at: . . . . Will ask . . . .

MINDFUL MAZE

Calm Ninja is out on a nature walk!
Count up each thing in the panel as
you go. It's okay if you get a bit lost,
it's all part of the fun!

START HERE

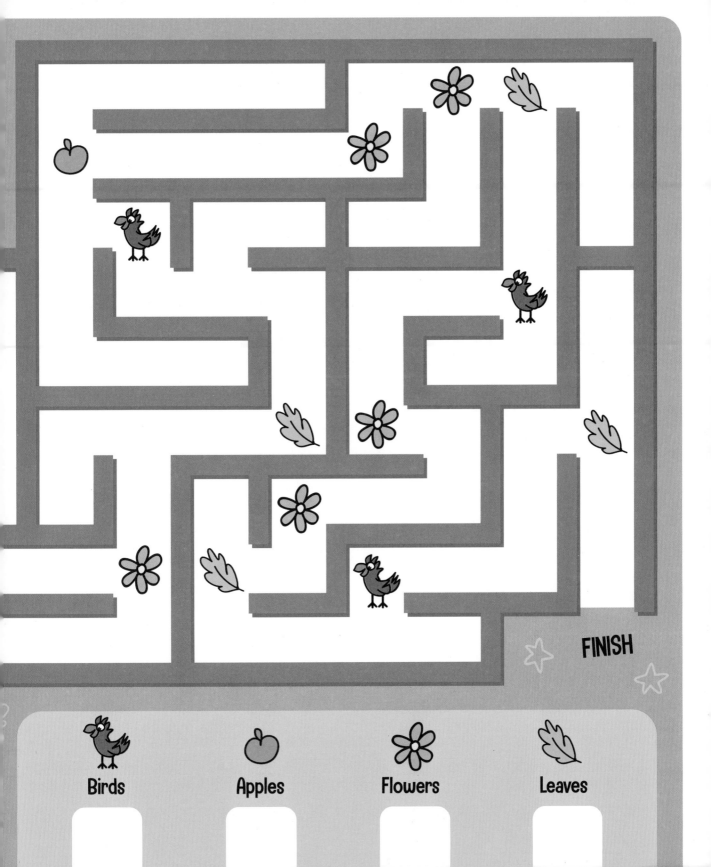

FINISH

Birds   Apples   Flowers   Leaves

SUPER SEQUENCES

Can you help Growth Mindset Ninja crack these puzzles? Circle what comes next in each row.

68

MISTAKES HELP ME GROW

MY GOALS

Write down something you'd like to learn or practice each week and fill in the grid. Draw a check under each day you practice it.

GOAL	Monday	Tuesday	Wednesday

**WHAT WAS
YOUR FAVORITE
THING YOU
LEARNED?**

Thursday	Friday	Saturday	Sunday

**WHICH GOAL
DID YOU ENJOY
THE LEAST?**

How did this activity
make YOU feel?

Add a thumbs-up or a
thumbs-down sticker here.

DOODLE TIME

Not only is drawing fun, but it's good for your brain, too. It helps build new connections and pathways, so keep exercising that muscle! Learn to draw Growth Mindset Ninja using this grid.

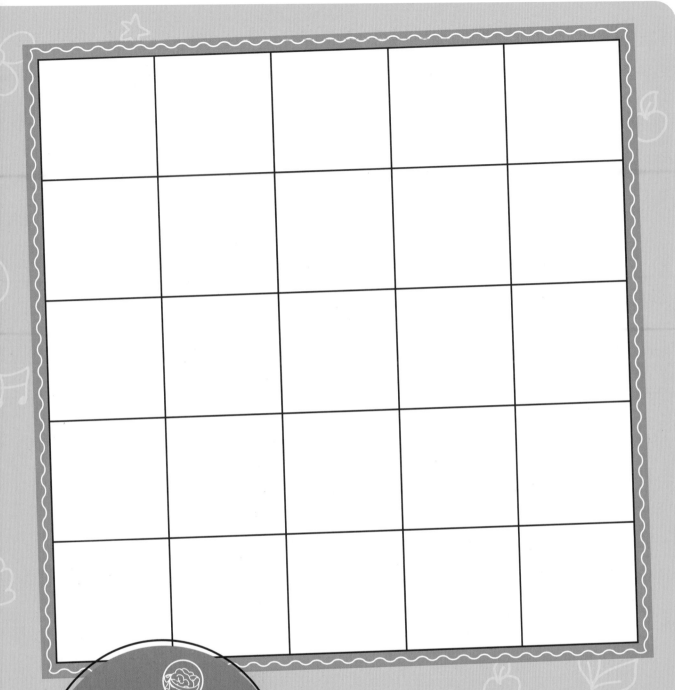

DRAWING IS GOOD FOR YOUR MENTAL HEALTH. IT ENCOURAGES YOUR BRAIN TO RELEASE ENDORPHINS TO HELP YOU FEEL GOOD.

How did this activity make YOU feel?

Add a thumbs-up or a thumbs-down sticker here.

WHICH NINJA NEXT?

Check out these patterns, then color in which ninja comes next.

A

MASKED NINJA

HANGRY NINJA

UNPLUGGED NINJA

B

GROWTH MINDSET NINJA

FOCUSED NINJA

FOCUSED NINJA

GROWTH MINDSET NINJA

C

SAD NINJA

SAD NINJA

HUMBLE NINJA

UNPLUGGED NINJA

SAD NINJA

ARROW MAZE

Smart Ninja has set Growth Mindset Ninja a tough challenge. Can you find your way through this maze by following the arrows?

FROM EACH ARROW YOU CAN MOVE TO ANY OF THE ARROWS IT'S POINTING TO, IN THE SAME ROW, COLUMN, OR DIAGONAL.

I believe in you, Growth Mindset Ninja!

→ START	→	↙	↓
←	↙	↗	↓
→	→	↗	↓
↙	↓	←	FINISH

FEELING OVERWHELMED?

No sweat—here's a few ideas for things you can do. Check off each one as you try it.

- [✓] Go for a walk

- [✓] Talk to a grown-up about how I feel

- [✓] Doodle things that make me happy

- [✓] Do some mindful coloring

- [✓] Tidy my room to create a calm space

- [✓] Write a letter for someone special

- [✓] Look at my favorite photos

- [✓] Do a silly dance

- [✓] Think about things I am good at

- [ ] Do some stretches

  ~~~~~~

- [ ] Accept that I can't be good at everything

  ~~~~~~

- [ ] Read a funny book

  ~~~~~~

- [ ] Write in a journal

  ~~~~~~

- [ ] Close my eyes and think positive thoughts

  ~~~~~~

- [ ] Talk to a friend

WRITE YOUR OWN IDEAS HERE.

How did this activity make YOU feel?

Add a thumbs-up or a thumbs-down sticker here.

EVERYONE TOGETHER

Can you complete the gang by using your stickers to finish the puzzle?

BELIEVE IN YOURSELF

Answers:

PAGE 10: THIS WAY

PAGE 16: TANGLED LINES

PAGE 17: ODD FISH OUT

1. B IS THE ODD ONE OUT.
2. C IS THE ODD ONE OUT.
3. B IS THE ODD ONE OUT.

PAGE 21: TONS OF TOYS

PAGES 22-23: JUST BREATHE

THERE ARE 8 NINJAS IN THE PICTURE

1. THERE ARE 3 YELLOW NINJAS IN THE SCENE. F
2. ONE NINJA IS NOT USING A MAT. T
3. ALL THE NINJAS LOOK CALM F

PAGES 24-25: MAKE IT MATCH

PAGE 26: WORD SEARCH

F	W	H	U	P	B	H	D	S	Z	P	C	S	W	E
U	G	V	X	B	A	T	N	V	A	G	Y	J	K	M
S	E	Q	Z	E	J	L	U	C	Z	B	Z	P	Y	L
B	N	U	W	L	I	A	P	R	A	C	T	I	C	E
P	C	Q	M	I	N	B	V	C	M	A	S	M	Y	A
K	O	Y	B	E	C	X	Z	N	B	L	H	P	A	R
L	U	K	J	V	H	G	F	D	I	A	M	R	N	N
V	R	L	K	E	H	G	F	D	T	D	C	O	U	I
O	A	W	Y	H	B	K	S	K	I	A	P	V	N	N
O	G	N	H	F	R	S	O	A	Q	H	U	E	J	G
W	E	Q	C	H	A	L	L	E	N	G	E	W	E	R
P	O	I	U	T	I	D	V	C	V	V	B	N	M	W
M	H	T	F	V	N	X	E	D	H	C	Z	C	V	L
E	R	T	Y	U	I	O	H	F	D	S	I	O	M	A
I	F	S	U	C	C	E	S	S	R	Y	J	V	C	A

PAGE 27: FEELING GOOD

PAGES 30-31: WHAT A MESS

PAGE 37: KEEP CALM

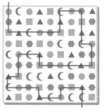

PAGE 42: FUN AT THE FAIR

1. B IS THE ODD ONE OUT.
2. C IS THE ODD ONE OUT.
3. D IS THE ODD ONE OUT.

PAGE 43: CRACK THE CODE

ANYTHING IS POSSIBLE
YOU NEVER KNOW UNTIL YOU TRY

PAGES 52-53: SKATE ON

PAGE 56: MATCHY MATCHY

D MATCHES THE BIG PICTURE.

PAGE 60: PAPER PLANE RACE

HELPFUL NINJA IS THE WINNER

PAGE 61: SUDOKU

PAGES 66-67: MINDFUL MAZE

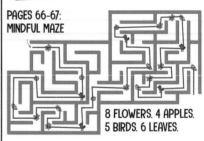

8 FLOWERS. 4 APPLES.
5 BIRDS. 6 LEAVES.

PAGE 68: SUPER SEQUENCES

A

B

C

PAGE 75: ARROW MAZE

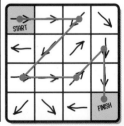